# CONTENTS

## Op. 68

## Op. 71

# Sailor's Song

Op. 68, No. 1

48664x

# Grandmother's Minuet

Op. 68, No. 2

Allegretto grazioso e leggierissimo

48664

# At Your Feet

Op. 68, No. 3

Poco Andante e molto espressivo

# Evening in the Mountains

Op. 68, No. 4

# Cradle Song

Op. 68, No. 5

Allegretto tranquillamente

# Melancholy Waltz

Tempo di Valse tranquillo

Op. 68, No. 6

Tempo I

# Once Upon a Time

# Summer Evening

Op. 71, No. 2

Allegretto tranquillamente

# Puck

Op. 71, No. 3

# Peace of the Woods

Op. 71, No. 4

# Halling

Allegro molto

Op. 71, No. 5

Allegro moderato e marcato

# Gone

Op. 71, No. 6

Andante doloroso

# Remembrances

Tempo di Valse

Op. 71, No. 7

# SCHIRMER'S LIBRARY
## OF MUSICAL CLASSICS

Vol. 1956

# EDVARD GRIEG

## Lyric Pieces

For Piano

Op. 68, Op. 71

Op. 12, Op. 38—Library Vol. 1952

Op. 43, Op. 47—Library Vol. 1953

Op. 54, Op. 57—Library Vol. 1954

Op. 62, Op. 65—Library Vol. 1955

Op. 68, Op. 71—Library Vol. 1956

ISBN 978-0-7935-4520-9

## G. SCHIRMER, Inc.

DISTRIBUTED BY

7777 W. BLUEMOUND RD. P.O. BOX 13819 MILWAUKEE, WI 53213

Printed in the U.S.A. by G. Schirmer, Inc.